BAMBOO DIARY

Copyright 2010 Library of Congress
ISBN: 978-0557-32174-2

For David, Judy, Julie, Wanda, Jennifer,
Melissa, Stuart, Brittany, and Sydney

This is dedicated to Pi Xiang *(P Shia ng)*.
A man of strong convictions and unwavering support,
Xiang represents a new age in China with traditional
ties to the past. He and I somehow share a connection
to the past and the future. He is, without a doubt,
my last angel.

For as long as I can remember events in my life come to me first in dreams. No matter when it will happen it usually comes to me first in the form of a dream. This neither frightens me nor does it make me think of myself as special in any way. It is as though pieces of a jigsaw puzzle finally fall in place when reality reflects the dream.

Once my husband asked me what I saw myself doing twenty years from that moment. Without any hesitation I answered working with children in a country far away. In the dream I was alone, but never shared that with him.

Twenty years later and divorced found me boarding a plane to teach at a university in China. The timing of the event seemed incredible.

At the time he asked me he was a Navy officer. We had been married about four years. I had three children from a previous marriage and was working as a bank executive. Often I have wondered how it was possible to dream something that was so far from reality at that time. I have tried to adjust to simply trust the dreams. If it happens, it happens.

Many years before when the children were little my first husband and I visited my parents who lived on the coast in Florida. One afternoon the children were playing in the sand on the beach. I rowed a small johnboat out to go fishing. The hot sun made me very sleepy. I don't remember falling asleep, but do remember dreaming.

Looking down from a hill I could see myself in the boat. It was as though I was two different people yet the same. Up on the high bank I wore a long gown. It was warm with the hot sun shining down on me. I was very much at home up on the hill and content. There were beautiful gardens all around me. It was shady next to the large house behind me. I was at peace with all around me.

Water was lapping up around the boat. Looking up I could see the children still playing in the sand. It must have only been minutes. Once inside I told my parents what had happened. Dad who was a college professor wanted to know if I had been into his Scotch. When I laughingly said no, he said perhaps it was too much sun and to rest then.

Forgetting it became impossible. Over the next six months or so, I drew out the house floor plan for anyone that would listen to my story. It was as though I knew every stone in the garden path, every flower, and was very much at home there.

When we returned for another visit at Christmas to my parents, my younger sister, Terri, and I set out in the car to try to find the place on the hill. She was as curious as I was about the incident.

We drove down several driveways in the direction I could remember while in the boat. Then we found it. The area was vacant and had been deserted for some time it seemed. There was an outline of a garden area left with many beautiful flowers still blooming there. The existing steps to the house were exactly as I knew they would be.

The steps and the outline in stone of the house was all that remained. It was exactly the same as in my drawing.

Tall lumbering pine and oak trees were still standing there that must have shaded the house long ago. Spanish moss draped some branches as a soft veil.

Once inside the house long ago I always turned to go to the left. It was cool and quiet there. Something was in the center of the room that I cannot see clearly. I only remember the coolness of the air and peacefulness.

It was comforting to know that it really did exist. On the way driving out we spotted a decaying wooden sign half buried in the bushes. It read *Sisters of Carmelite Hospital.* Perhaps in another life and another time I lived there. I will never know for sure. From that day on I learned to trust the dreams.

Sharing a quiet moment with my best friend, Libby, before I went to China also came in a dream. She and I were actually able to do so while driving to New Orleans to the airport. She always encouraged me to follow my dream. Without her support I would never have had the courage for such an adventure by myself.

She is a modern Doris Day. Her blonde hair and style have always been the most perfect coiffure since I have known her. Somehow everyday she manages to make it look absolutely beautiful. She is always smiling and cheerful. Her love of animals is reflected in her many dogs she has rescued and brought home to live in her house. She is the most generous and gentle soul. I consider her to be my best friend and as close as a sister.

Weeks before I had given my children everything I owned in the farm house. They would take all the possessions I had accumulated over forty years. It was theirs to do with as they wished.

My son, David, came in from Texas with his wife, Judy, and two grandchildren who are young adults now, Melissa and Stuart. Julie and her partner, Wanda, drove up from Key West. Jennifer, my youngest daughter, and her two daughters, Brittany and Sydney, lived with me and would take whatever the others didn't want. It didn't seem fair to make the children wait until I died to inherit things.

David, works as a director for an international computer company while his talented partner, Judy, has her own home-based business. They seem happy with their lives. I don't see them or my grandchildren in Texas very often. Everyone is always so busy working or going to college. Melissa and Stuart have grown up. They have developed into mature, caring adults.

I witnessed Brittany and Sydney growing up, but very little of Melisa and Stuart's lives have I shared since they lived away. It is no one's fault. It simply has been that way. That is the one regret of my life.

Julie is a probation officer. She has a lovely partner, Wanda. They have a deep commitment for each other. We all consider Wanda a loving member of our family. Julie came out about being gay while she was in college. I am proud for her for being honest about her life, and that she has found someone she loves. Julie is extremely dependable.

Jennifer, my youngest daughter, is an excellent cook. In fact, Jennifer, Judy, Julie and Wanda are all good cooks. Jennifer is also one of the hardest working people I have ever known.

She is still searching for her future, but loves her two daughters, Brittany and Sydney. Sometimes, on Friday nights they would turn on old rock and roll songs on the radio, and slide across the kitchen floor dancing in their socks as they baked delicious cookies, or pumpkin bread.

They planned to stay in the farm house while I was gone. If they decided to move I would rent it out.

Brittany and Sydney shared my life for many years. I have watched them grow since they were born. Brittany is creative and daring. Sydney is a happy child. She wakes up happy. She chattered with me every morning. We drove the others crazy with our early morning conversations since they are late sleepers and definitely not morning people.

None of them said they were concerned about my being so far away. They wanted to make sure I was doing something that made me happy. It felt as though a paintbrush had swiped away and painted over my life. It was a new time now, a new beginning.

In New Orleans at the airport I kissed my dear friend goodbye. Walking barefoot from the security check I left with two suitcases containing everything I possessed. At sixty-two I was beginning a new life one that I had dreamed about years before.

The flight to China was nineteen hours. My fellow passenger was a Chinese man who had been in one of the first groups to graduate from college after the Cultural Revolution. He talked to me for most of the flight. I learned he and his wife had a son going to school at John Hopkins University. After college the man had accepted a job with the airlines and was transferred to the United States. He only returned each year to visit his parents. He was the first Chinese man that ever spoke with me in person. My other contacts had been by internet and mail. He was polite and respectful. I wondered if all Chinese men were like him.

The flight gave me time to reflect what I was undertaking. Traveling and going to new places has always been exciting to me. When I was young my father was in the Air Force so the family got to see new places. He became a history professor when he retired from the military. Mom was a wonderful and supportive partner to him throughout her life. For the most part wherever Dad went she took us along too.

They were both gone now. As the eldest of four sisters, all with families, I was leaving that world behind temporarily. My sister, Nancy, would be the matriarch now.

Before I began school we stayed in St. Louis with my mother's parents while Dad was off fighting in World War II. We would pack big boxes of home-made goodies for him. We would spend hours popping bags and bags of real popcorn to pack in-between the items. He was in North Africa and then flew into China over the snow-capped mountains of Tibet to help transport Chinese troops to India and back.

I began kindergarten in Okinawa. It was during the Korean conflict. When there were air raid warnings the teachers would walk us up single-file to some caves in the hills above the school. Inside the cave the walls were black and wet. Some of the children would softly cry. I could never understand why because I thought it was so exciting. We would stand there safe inside the cave and stare at the light from outside.

After my children were born their father and I went to Austria and Germany for vacation during Oktoberfest. We stayed at the Munich Hilton, and toured the city. We also traveled through beautiful tiny hamlets in Germany and Austria. It was October and snowing in the Alps. The beautiful castles and narrow-cobbled streets were treasures waiting to be explored.

We went to a former concentration camp in Germany and visited the museum honoring the Jewish families and others that were put to death. Some of the trees standing there now were there during that time I remembered thinking. There was a huge poster of a young mother holding the hand of two little girls. I went to sit outside on the steps after seeing it and cried. I had two little girls then as well.

It was also shortly after the killing of Jewish athletes at the Olympics. It was the first time I went through and airport where they used the wand to trace the outline of your body for weapons. It was the first time I remember thinking maybe the world was not as safe as I always imagined.

As we approached China the airline served a meal of noodles in a cup. Thinking it was a joke I looked up to the smiling faces of the other passengers. I was expecting at least one good last western meal. When over one hundred people make a sucking sound eating noodles in soup it can be deafening. Navigating the chopsticks and soup without embarrassing myself was a challenge. I remember thinking I was going to starve.

Going through customs in the Beijing airport I was soaking wet. The heat was intense. There was no air conditioning it the terminal it seemed. No one else appeared to be bothered by it except me. An older man in an Islamic type cap turned around to me in the long line and handed me a tissue to wipe the perspiration running down my face. It was a simple, but kind and charitable act. Okay, if I didn't starve I would sweat to death.

The walk through customs and the terminal to get to my next flight was probably the longest distance I had walked in years. Normally I would walk ten feet out the front door, and be in my car.

Getting my luggage collected, through customs, and then to next flight on time was actually simple. I saw a young male porter eager for business. I paid him four hundred Yuan and told him what I needed to do. He made it happen in record time. It was probably not the most money he has ever made on one transaction, but definitely worth every cent to me.

A tall, lanky young man named Henry from the foreign office met me at the airport in the Wuhan to escort me to the university. It was raining when we landed there. The windows in the car began to fog over. The only way the driver and my companion would figure out how to solve the problem was to turn on the heat. It was August. It was late when we arrived at my new apartment tired, hungry and extremely hot.

I slept for the first twenty four hours there which caused the foreign office some concern. They had tried to call me, but the telephone wasn't working.

In my dreams.....

> *It was snowing heavily in the mountains. He and I walked most of the morning. The horses were tired, and needed rest. We did too. We had ridden all night to try and distance ourselves from the guards.*
>
> *If they found us they would take us back. Going back meant death. We could never go back. Never again would I be able to see my mother or sisters. We needed to find shelter before nightfall. The wind began to howl as snow billowed down upon us.*
>
> *He saw the opening to the cave before I did. Guiding the horses he led us up the mountain towards the small opening in the mountainside. It was concealed well from the path below. The*

horses snorted heavily inside the warmth of the cave.

There was a small pile of wood left over inside from another traveler's visit. The snow had blanketed the mountain so there would be no dry wood to find outside.

Try to rest he said to me as he began to build a fire. I slid down beside a large rock near the firewood pulling my wet robe up around me tighter. It was very cold. I began to relax as the flames from the fire grew higher. I remember the outline of his face and body against the fire light as I drifted off to sleep.

The sounds coming from inside the cave woke me. He was moving the horses back farther inside so they could not be heard by anyone passing below. He had found some dried grass for them to eat. There was a small pool of water further inside so they could be watered too. He filled our water bags as much as possible and returned to sit by the fire.

He closed his eyes as the fire danced in from of him. He knew the guards would have to stop their search as nightfall approached. Maybe for a few hours there would be no chase or no fight. For a few hours we would be out of the storm, and could rest. Slowly, he closed his eyes.

Surely these were dreams of a time long ago…yet I will never be sure.

Henry bought me some water, apples and bread to eat until I could get to the store.

The next morning I looked out back through my third story windows and saw tall willowy bamboo and oak trees. Everything was green, and delicate. I could see mountains in the distance through a mist. It was more magical to think of it as mist rather than pollution. So this is China I remember thinking.

Going to the grocery store for the first time was fairly easy. Henry and his sister, who spoke English and her twin girls, accompanied me. Everyone stared as though I was from Mars. Previously there had been few white females in the city.

I found some foods and products recognizable. The quantity I bought caused quite a reaction among the other customers. They shop daily for fresh vegetables. I, on the other hand, use the volume shopping method to be happy. They were staring in my basket seeing what the strange foreigner bought.

School wasn't going to begin for a few weeks so I had time to accumulate to the heat, and get settled. My neighbor, Clementine, a beautiful teacher from Cameroon was afraid of the afternoon lightening. I suggested we get a bottle of wine for the storms. It did help. She had been in the country for a year and had taught at a high school previously. Her husband, a professor in Cameroon, would try and join her the following year. He had been her teacher in college. She had fallen in love with him then.

Whenever she and I would shop together we caused traffic to stop. Since she was dark ebony, and I was as white as a ghost so we made quite a pair. She asked me not to make eye contact with other customers because it caused them to come closer. I couldn't help talking or waving to the small children.

A car ran upon a curb once simply because the driver was staring at me. I couldn't tell if it was flattering or just curiosity. It never ceased no matter where I went. I knew how celebrities felt finally when others went past and took cell phone pictures of me whenever they saw me. I always said to myself- just smile and be polite. Most people were just curious.

Adjusting to the food and differences in hygiene in restaurants was difficult. The Asian food we had in America was simply not the same food. They had never heard of egg rolls. Also they could eat any type of green thing that grew in ground even if it was what we considered to be a weed. Very little meat, and lots of vegetables and fruit was their secret to being so thin.

Everyday I was surrounded by extremely thin people who gave me advice on how to improve my health. It was intended with kindness. I would have preferred the same type of silence we give each other in the US when we are overweight.

Some months later while shopping with a student a female in the grocery store walked up behind and put her hands on my bottom measuring how big she thought it was. She used the Chinese word for fat to the handsome male student with me. He sweetly said it doesn't matter what size you are if you are healthy. It is difficult to know who to believe at times-the handsome young male or the little old lady with her hands on your fat butt.

I had dreams of fried pork chops. After a while I reasoned that you could fry the germs off any meat if you just cooked it long enough. Seeing the pork, chicken or beef lying out on a table in the sun waiting to be sold during the day was difficult to endure. Eventually, I overcame my concerns about flies, and everyone touching it knowing that enough heat could eradicate any germs.

Also in the Asian culture age is an important distinction. I was never asked my age as a social question until I came to China. But I was asked by everyone I met. It is considered a sign of respect. I never thought of myself as old until I was treated as an older person.

Students told me most people did not work past fifty or fifty five. For someone as old as sixty-two to be working was miraculous. A grandmother's job, they said, in China is to stay home and take care of the grandchild. Also, due to the population they need to make way for younger adults to have jobs.

My four grandchildren were almost grown. They had their parents, my children, to help them. I was only away not dead. We were only a phone call or email apart.

When classes began I was told there would be monitors. Not quite sure what that meant I discovered they are the student leaders of the class who make sure the other students do their homework and behave. Everyone it seemed was responsible for everyone else. The collective society was definitely different that the independent society I had grown up with in the US.

The first day of class I met him. He walked up to me before class and introduced himself. I am Sammy, he said. He was tall for a Chinese man, I thought. I did not think most of the Chinese men I had met before him were handsome, but he was different. I remember his face most of all, and his black hair.

He was a freshman in my class. His English was spoken softly. He had the most amazing smile. It must have taken great courage for him to walk up to me and boldly introduce himself. Most students were too shy to speak first.

Later he told me he had first said hello in a restaurant as he passed by and I vaguely remember it. My most singular initial memory of him is in the classroom. He also could not really understand many things I said during those first few months of the semester. My southern accent was new to him.

I had asked two of my best students if they could help me with learning Chinese during that first semester. Sammy was one of the students. I had written it down because I didn't want there to be any misunderstanding. I would pay each student to tutor me for two hours per week if they had time. I thought this would give them some extra money and help me at the same time.

Each student had a different approach. Sammy wanted to do normal things such as cooking and began there. So he came to my apartment and we cooked. Actually, he cooked and I watched. He taught me the names of the vegetables first. He was an amazingly good cook. Sometimes he would sing Chinese songs softly while he cooked. My job was to clean the kitchen afterwards and listen.

Sometimes he and I went shopping in town or down the road to the market. He began to think of himself as my assistant. He truly became that too helping me in communicating to other Chinese what I needed.

The other young man, Rick, was an extremely good student. He had little accent and spoke English well. He was kind and polite. He and I went shopping for shoes or to the dress maker. His father was an animal doctor and he came from a larger family.

Sammy was an only child, an emperor child, as they call them. He lived, when he wasn't at the school campus, with his parents and grandfather in a small city about an hour away. His hometown is well-known for the lakes and fish farming they do there.

At the end of that semester Rick and I stopped his class. He was becoming busy at college, and needed the time to study. He had been very helpful.

Another male student had been visiting with me during the semester. This young man was going to India to study. He had already graduated from college and had been auditing my classes that first semester. He had never really even spoken to me until we met at a party at another teacher's home one evening. I had wondered who he was, but it was not unusual for students to audit classes.

Odom was friendly and handsome. Much older than the other students he seemed like one of the Chinese teachers. He came to see me almost daily for months.

Sometimes Sammy would question me about the other man. I thought they were joking when they would see who could outstay the other one at my apartment.

Once they left my apartment at the same time. Then Odom told him he had left something so he came back and visited for much longer. It became a game between them.

Odom would leave for India in the summer. Sammy just bided his time it seemed. Both were funny and friendly. Both were very intelligent. They tugged at my heart in different ways.

Sammy was many things though that Odom was not. Sammy was not afraid of anything. He had self-confidence even though he was younger. He seemed more determined and focused. He could talk about his feelings.

The first day it snowed in China that winter was on January 12th.We had a birthday party the night before for Jack, one of the male Chinese teachers. He said no one had ever given him a party before so this had been a special occasion. I had bet one of the Swedish teachers it would snow the next day. She paid off with a nice bottle of red wine the next morning.

That morning Rick and his three roommates came over early to my apartment. They tried to coax Odom and me to come out for pictures and to play in the snow. Odom was not happy, but he went. He just has gotten warm from being outside in the snow earlier when he walked to my apartment.

Rick and I made a snowman then started a snowball fight. Soon it seemed as though most of the students still on campus joined in. Spring break was beginning so most students were going home. We had teams fighting other teams. It was glorious.

It reminded me of when I was a child and played in the snow with my cousins in St. Louis at my grandmother's home. It was the first time I had seen snow in years. It was a wonderful day I will never forget.
That afternoon as I napped I dreamed:

> *I dreamed that I lived in a snowy place in a large house. In my home lived an elderly Indian grandfather that I cared for. He sat by a fire and rocked in a chair softly singly Indian chants.*
> *His grandson was a doctor. He did not live with us, but stayed close by so he could help with his grandfather. He was handsome and tall. He was a gentle and caring man. He was my soul mate.*

During the semester break it is called Spring Festival in China. Everyone goes home or travels to be with family. It had snowed for several days and traffic was becoming a problem.

Odom left for home as did most of the students. It would be quiet for a few weeks without them.

Sammy knocked on my door one night and said he couldn't get home because of the snow. The buses had stopped running due to the severe weather. The roads were icing over. He had stayed longer at school because he was working a part-time job. His father wasn't aware of his job. His dormitory was closing. He had no place to stay he said.

I invited him in and called the foreign office to let them know a student was stranded and staying with me. Sammy called his parents and let them know too.

Henry came over and stayed most evenings to make sure nothing was happening. I thought that was funny because of our age difference. The two male foreign teachers were gone so he couldn't stay with them.

One day the snow had let up a little. Sammy's father called and told him to come home for the traditional spring festival meals. Sammy's father made him quit his job when he found out. He packed and left by bus to go home. We had become good friends during his visit.

One morning before he left I was typing on the computer. I looked up and not twenty feel away from me he was curled up under my white fluffy down comforter. One of life's wonderful distractions lay sleeping so peacefully. Sometimes you have to be grateful for many things including snow.

Henry invited me to his family's home for the holidays. One of the Swedish foreign teachers and I went to share the holiday meals with them. It was a warm, wonderful event shared by all of Henry's relatives. He has six brothers and sisters which is not common in China. All of them are teachers or doctors. His parents had both been teachers. They had fireworks, and special foods they valued. It was a very exciting experience. His father wrote out for me a beautiful Chinese poem. It still hangs on my wall.

They give red envelopes to the children as a present. I gave Henry a red envelope which he in turn passed on to his twin nieces. I was grateful to have given it to him so he could share it with them.

My first spring festival in China was a special time. I was no longer a tourist or passerby in this country. I began to feel a part of something much bigger than just myself or my family. I was also connected now to the people in China that had become part of my life.

During that first summer I went home to visit returning in August. I took gifts home and brought some special things back for various students and teachers. It was great to have spent time with my own family and friends during that summer. I visited with Libby almost daily at her job, and spent the afternoons swimming at my daughter's apartment pool. To lie out and tan was absolutely something you did not do in China. Most women carry umbrellas to keep the sun off of them for fear of tanning. I loved every minute of it.

Sammy and I came from totally different cultures. We were ages apart. Somehow we had become as close as family to one another that year. We supported each other financially and emotionally. For most of the time he acted as the primary support. He was the caretaker in our relationship. For the first time in my life I did not have to assume that role.

He was an integral part of my life that fall. It was not expected or planned. I could not imagine how different my life would have been without him. They should put that in brochures about teaching abroad. There are many unexpected joys about teaching in Asia.

He had moved into my apartment during the fall. First I would find he had left a few things, maybe shoes or some books. Then I noticed he was beginning to nest as I jokingly told him. He found a reason to always leave things in my apartment.

Sometimes he would use my computer line for his laptop and would stay overall night working on it. He started making a pallet on the floor if he worked late.

Think I was in denial about him living with me. All of his stuff was there, he showered there, he slept there, he cooked there, and his friends called or visited him there. I keep thinking it was just temporary since he had another apartment that he chose not to go to for whatever reason.

Later we became organized. He got a bed and a portable closet for his clothes. There was no pretense between us. He was living there. We tried to be discrete. I was a teacher and he was my student.

We were very close friends, but don't think anyone believed that story. His parents knew he lived there. So did most of the other foreign teachers. He and I had no secrets between us.

That October holiday we decided to go to Wudang Mountain. Sammy made the arrangements with a travel agent. We planned to spend the night before in Wuhan.

We took the train to Wuhan which is about an hour away. In October apparently everyone travels so finding a taxi when we got to Wuhan took an hour waiting in line.

Chinese people are not usually good about standing in queue. They constantly try to go to the first of the line. It is something you get used to in time. It is simply a cultural difference.

Our hotel rooms were several stories up. Actually the outside was a regular cell phone business. You had to walk all the way to the back of this big warehouse to see the stairs to the hotel entrance. I would never have found it on my own so I wad grateful he went with me.

This was my first experience in a Chinese hotel. It was a modest price for the rooms so I was prepared for economy features. The floor was wooden with no rugs at all. A single bed with a tiny blanket was centered the room. There was a strange coat rack that served as a closet. The room size was the size of my bathroom at my farm. It did have a western style bathroom so I really didn't care about anything else.

Sammy had friends he wanted to meet so they went shopping while I slept. That night we ate at Pizza Hut. Yes, they have chain restaurants such as McDonalds, KFC, and Pizza Hut. Only the food served has some differences in that it is spicy compared to what we normally would eat in the west.

The next morning we went to catch the travel coach that would take us to Wudang. Chinese buses are designed for the size of average Chinese person. In general, they are shorter in stature than westerners. Sammy is taller than most so he was cramped sitting there for six hours.

My knees felt crippled from being so confined. It is just something you have to adjust to if you want to travel.

We traveled past areas that slowly became small hills and then mountains. In traveling to Wudang we never saw a factory or any industry. There were no airplanes flying overhead. It seemed strange to me after the bustling city of Wuhan. The miles of farmland were still green even though it was October.

After about six hours the bus finally pulled into the entrance area. I was amazed. This is what Tibet must look like I thought. The mountains were beautiful. The buildings looked like the travelogues from Tibet. The air was crisp and clean. It was a beautiful sunny day for sightseeing.

We left the bus and went through the entrance. Since I was the only westerner there were no translators so Sammy had to translate for fours days. I knew he was tired when the guide would speak for fifteen minutes and then he would tell me they didn't say anything important. It felt strange not to be able to read any signs or brochures or to understand what people were saying. My ability in understanding Chinese was still limited.

We met a couple from Israel who stopped me and asked if I understood anything there. I explained that Sammy was translating for me. They found it difficult to understand where or what things were there without any language other than Chinese posted. It is a UNESCO site, but it is also a pilgrimage for many Chinese. There were thousands of people visiting this beautiful area since it was a holiday.

I was excited about going up to the temples on top of the mountain. It would be my first time seeing something as old and sacred. It was truly a spiritual experience.

We took another bus up the mountain. Then you can walk up about nine hundred stairs or take a cable car. Sammy wanted to walk, but I pleaded with him to go with me on the cable car. He had never been on one but he agreed. About halfway up I was turning around to admire the beautiful view when I saw he was rigid. He was speaking loudly when he asked me not to move around because it made the car shake. I believe I heard him praying softly.

He decided he would walk down the mountain while I took the car back again. For some reason he changed his mind on the way back. He had overcome his fear of it. He called one of his friends on his cell phone on the trip down to share with them what he was doing. He was the first in his family to ride a cable car.

There are no words sufficient to accurately describe how beautiful the temples are at Wudang Mountain. You can physically feel the past, and all the history of this ancient and spiritual place. It was incredible for both of us.

Coming back from there made me listen to my inner voice. Somehow the trip made me want to listen. Maybe it is spiritual after all. It felt that way to me.

I also saw life as it has been for the past centuries carried out by ordinary Asian people. I saw men and women working in fields small and large with rudimentary tools. No work boots and overalls were donned, just regular clothes. Water buffalo worked in some of the fields. These animals are enormous yet appear docile.

We drove for hours and never saw any type of industry only farmers laboring in their fields. There was no John Deere equipment anywhere to be seen. They used large hoes or square shovels to work the fields. Some were squatting in the fields pulling clumps of crops out with their hands.

The air was clear near the mountains, but as we neared any level patch of land you could see the smoke. The sky was thick and there was no blue left in it. Slash and burn farming methods still exists. We passed the haze of burning fields as the farmers have prepared them for centuries there. No store bought fertilizers, or chemicals available or affordable here.

There were some carts piled high with wood or crops led by water buffalo. Men and women toiled hunched over for hours preparing for the next crop.

The most beautiful patchwork of gardens and crops exist in any space between the mountains and on any level surface. They plant in terraces. The soil is a rich brown shade of earth. Rows of tea plants hug the sides of mountains. Irrigation canals exist in every field to some degree.

There were streams, lakes, or rivers all along the way. Even at high altitudes there was an abundance of water for farming or fishing.

These fields support the families that work them. It provides whatever food and money they have for the year. They have no other jobs. They sell in small open markets what they cannot use. Nothing is wasted. Items we consider weeds are sold as vegetables here. I have eaten them.

It is not the commercialized farming we know in the west. No huge combines drive down the fields. The size of each field is actually quite small in comparison to what we are used to seeing. It is done primarily by manual labor as it has been done for centuries. There is no reason to change it because it works.

Houses had the front ground covered in corn leveled out to dry. Bright yellow stocks of corn also hung across the roofs of the homes as you would hang Christmas lights.

You could see older men guiding goats from one field to another or to their homes. Goats in groups of six to ten ate the stubble of crops and added fertilizer along the way to the next field.

Even though we were driving along at a high speed it almost seemed as though time stopped for those few hours. It gave me time to witness a way of life I will never know or barely understand.

It is raining in those fields now. The same rain that is falling outside my window is the only connection I will have to those farmers. But for a few hours I listened with my eyes and saw them and will never forget them.

Sammy was sleeping next to me on the bus. I leaned my head next to his shoulder and fell asleep too.

As the bus rocked along I continued my strange dream…

> *The time passed quickly it seemed. The fire was smoldering when I awoke. The horses had rested. My robe was no longer wet. I felt hungry, but knew we had no time to find food. He stirred as I woke up. The sun was rising. We could see it from inside the cave. The snow had stopped falling, but still covered everything.*
>
> *We must go he said. I rose and walked to the entrance of the*

cave .What will happen this day I wondered to myself. I wanted to believe it was truly possible to escape.

He readied the horses for travel. Leading them down the mountain trail they seemed nervous. The path was slippery and steep still deep with snow.

My cloth shoes were wet as I mounted the horse. Another day of being cold and wet laid ahead I knew. That was nothing to complain about. At least I am alive and free now I thought. Leading the way down the hill ahead of me was the man I loved.

My love for him would cost us our lives if the guards caught up with us. I nudged the horse forward into the snowy path.

I used to tell Sammy he was going to make someone a wonderful husband one day. We joked that we must have known each other in another lifetime for us to have that feeling of depth in our relationship. I told him he was my last angel.

My second spring festival in China I was invited to stay at Sammy's home with his family. His mother had come and stayed with us for a few days before and we accompanied her back to their home. Sammy was treating her to get a permanent in her hair. She had seen mine a few months before and wanted to get one as well. She is a beautiful woman with untiring energy.

Sammy is tall and handsome like his father. His father had been a twin who was adopted when he was a child. The home they live in belongs to his father. The moment I met Sammy's grandfather I knew that he was the grandfather in my dream. The puzzle fell into place. The grandfather was elderly and was cared for in his home. He would rock in his chair and sing softly to himself. His grandson was tall and handsome. He was the same color as the man in my dreams. His grandson, Sammy, was the man in my dreams.

It was my first experience to stay in a home of a Chinese family. They were gracious and warm. The mother and father cooked many delicious dishes for the holiday.

Once when I walked into their bathroom I saw there were fish swimming in a large bucket. Sammy said they were raising them as a treat for the holiday. They were a special type of fish that had few bones. Sammy's father had gotten them especially for me since he knew I didn't like bones in fish. They must have cost a lot of money.

His parents were ordinary workers, and not a wealthy family. I was very honored that they had gone to such lengths to include me in their family celebration.

His mother's relatives lived next door. His parents had grown up next door to each other as children and married as adults. I asked Sammy once how his father and mother met. He told me he could never ask them such a personal question. In his culture, he had never been told he was loved or told his parents he loved them. He never remembered being kissed by his parents. Yet he knew without a doubt he was loved by them.

Once on father's day Sammy had called home to talk to his father. He told me later he wanted to tell him he loved him, but was too shy. I often wondered how he could be so open and affectionate with me, but still observe his traditional customs with anyone Chinese. It must be difficult to live in two worlds.

I decided to teach at another university for my third year. Sammy would be graduating within the year. I wanted to see more of China. Our living together seemed ideal, yet was problematic at times. He would not be my student the next year. In the two years I had known him, I never thought of him as a student. He was simply the man of the house and took care of things. I felt pampered.

Later I realized he had been hurt because I never asked his feelings about my decision. For so long I had made my own decisions without anyone else to rely on. So naïve as it seems, it never occurred to me he would have any emotions about it. My leaving meant changes in his world too.

My purse had been stolen one evening when we went out to supper with Federico, an Italian teacher. It contained my passport, keys and all my money. Losing the keys and money was the easy part. Losing the passport became a difficult experience.

The embassy was helpful and quick in assisting me. I made an appointment to go to Beijing to the embassy to get the replacement.

Sammy went with me. He made the arrangement for the hotel. He booked one room to save money he said. Know how careful he was in spending money or worrying about my money it seemed to make sense.

He had taken a driver training class earlier that spring. He got his driver's license. He asked a friend from his training class to help take us to the train station in Wuhan for our trip to Beijing. Realizing neither one of them had much driving experience I was a bit nervous. We had to be at the train station at a specific time or we would miss my appointment with the embassy.

I sat in the back seat on the trip so Sammy could sit with his friend. She was driving then pulled over so Sammy could practice. It began to rain very hard. Once when I looked up there were three hands on the steering wheel. I tried not to look up again until we stopped. It made me too nervous.

We were to have another driver part of the way. This person was supposed to know how to get to the train station in Wuhan. As we approached the change over we had a flat tire. Through the pouring rain, Sammy ran to find the other driver. He came back and collected me and our luggage. He was soaking wet and nervous we would miss our train. The female driver was getting the tire changed when we left.

The other driver, a young man, must have taken race car driving lessons. I have never been driven so fast through a major city. When we arrived minutes before the train was to leave, Sammy and the driver began running with our luggage with me trailing behind. We were all soaking wet from the rain. Thank goodness the train was late in leaving. This does not happen often, but was a blessing this day.

As we boarded the train Sammy had me sit down in the conductor's seat to catch my breath. He was exhausted and wet. We made our way to our seats to find a fight ensuing within a family about moving out of our seats. I was traumatized by the time we sat down. He had tried so hard to make everything perfect I knew he was upset.

When we arrived in Beijing it was night time and cold. Since it had been hot when we left Wuhan neither of us brought a jacket. The rain was coming in almost vertically with the wind blowing so hard.

As we passed the large poster of Chairman Mao across from Tiananmen Square I knew we were finally there. We could see it even though it was raining as we drove by in the taxi.

The hotel was beautiful and modern. Bright blue neon lights glimmered up and down part of the structure. Hotel staff eagerly greeted up and showed us to our room. The room was absolutely lovely.

I tried to explain to Sammy there are things the hotel puts out for guests to take and use such as samples of shampoo, toothbrushes, etc. He thought I was stealing things from the hotel. I laughed so hard I cried when he told me. He couldn't understand why we would take those things if we didn't need them.

There were condoms in the night table beside the bed. I took those as a gag gift for one of the other teachers. Sammy was appalled. He said he would tell his mother to hide things at their home in case I wanted to take them.

The next morning we went to see some sites in Beijing and shop before the embassy appointment. I found wonderful souvenir shops. He was upset I was buying things with my own money because I didn't need them. I tried to explain the concept of shopping American style. We often buy things we don't need, but want.

At lunch there was a beautiful Muslim restaurant he wanted to try. We shopped for awhile then went back to the restaurant at noon. They brought out a beautiful copper hot pot for our table with all the dishes accompanying it. Normally he did all the ordering, but I wanted to look at the menu too. I saw one or two things I thought would taste good and asked him to order those as well.

The meal was delicious. About half way through he looked up at me and said I know all your bad habits and can't live with you anymore.

I thought to myself what just happened. I thought we were having a wonderful meal. We can't live together anymore, okay mister. I said fine. We stopped eating. I wanted to go back to the hotel. I was furious.

Once we got back to the hotel he turned off the room lights so he could take a nap. I sat there and cried. Who was this twenty year old to tell me he knew my bad habits. I tried to think what in the world was his talking about.

We never fought really. He constantly tried to get me to eat and act as he did. I had tired before to explain to him we came from different worlds with different ways of doing things.

My appointment with the embassy was that afternoon. I told him I was going to ask the hotel to cancel the room for that night and we would go back home early so he could pack up and leave. He got out of bed and came over and tried to joke with me. I was in no joking mood by then. I never tried to criticize him intentionally.

He was upset I never finished all my vegetables and wasted food he said. He hated that I wasted my own money. He was worried he wouldn't make enough money to take care of me. He worried when I stayed up and worked on the computer or couldn't sleep. I hadn't asked him about leaving the university. All of this came tumbling out. He was upset the train trip had been a trip from hell. He tried so hard to take care of everything.

I explained to him I didn't expect things to be perfect or for him to have to take care of everything. I never dreamed he would ever worry about some of those things. I had supported myself for so long that I never thought of someone else doing it for me. I felt drained.

We dressed and left for the embassy. Everything was taken care of in fifteen minutes it seemed. I had done all the paperwork in advance. My new passport would be mailed to me. Sammy got to see inside the American Embassy. It was my first time inside one too.

Afterwards we went shopping for jackets. It was still cold and windy. He found one, but clothes for women in China are small sizes. I had a dressmaker near the college make most of my clothes. So I froze as we walked around.

We did stay that night at the hotel. We were able to joke again finally.

The next morning when we went to check out I noticed Sammy closely examining the bill. I was several feet away from him looking out the window. All of a sudden I heard him yell across the lobby in front of everyone that they hotel charged thirty Yuan for the condoms.

I died laughing as I walked towards the elevator telling him to pay the bill. I couldn't believe he didn't just pay for it quietly. No one would have thought anything about it. Now everyone in the lobby thought we used the condoms. I guess if you stay in the same hotel room using the condom wasn't so hard to believe.

The trip home was uneventful. For that we were both grateful. We took a bus from Wuhan back to the university. We were both exhausted from the trip. He never moved out until I did that summer.

I kept trying to focus on moving to a larger university and larger city. I tried not to think about how different both our lives would be shortly. Two other teachers would travel with me to the new school. Nick, a young teacher I had taught with previously from England, would be teaching there with me. The other friend, Federico from Italy, was going to travel more before he left for Oxford at the end of summer.

Sammy's parents rented a car and came to say goodbye the morning I left. His parents are wonderful people. He would go home with them for the summer break.

I had given him things for his apartment that I couldn't take with me. He had carried those things over beforehand. We had a few private moments to hug and kiss goodbye. I was afraid I would cry, but he said he couldn't deal with that so I tried not to do so.

It was a huge expense for his parents to rent a car. It was a very special honor for them to come and say goodbye to me. They didn't speak English, but we were able to communicate about most things. I hugged them as I left.

I was to drive by van with the two other teachers to the train station. Some students had come to say goodbye. I felt sad. Henry would go with us to the train station. He had mentioned he would like to have a zippo lighter some time before. I found one shopping and gave it to him as I left. I looked back at Sammy and his parents talking with the other students as we drove away. He and I waved goodbye.

Previously I had said goodbye to the two other teachers there that had become my friends for the past two years. Wayne, a special friend and a Canadian, had taught at the university for six years. He had found a Chinese teacher he would marry. The other, Freddie, from France, was a handsome young man all the female students adored. I found him to be sensitive and a good friend.

Nick, Federico, and I took a sleeper train to Shanxi Datong

which was my next school. It would take almost twenty-four hours, but was a direct train so it was convenient. The bed was very comfortable. I had mailed most of my things ahead of time so had very little to carry with me.

The guys were funny to travel with and kept me laughing. It helped to ease the shock of realizing Sammy was no longer there with me. I had made a choice. He needed to have a normal college life, and so did I. We would always think of each other as family. I hoped we would see each other again.

It was easy to fall to sleep with the train gently moving along.

Inside my robe tucked close to my heart was a cloth he had brought to me from the Silk Road travelers to the west. Never before had I seen such beautiful embroidery work with vivid colors, and texture.

There were animals on it that he said lived in those countries far away. He told me of the fierce golden and black striped tiger whose claws could pull a man apart .The tiger was as tall as a man when it stood up on its hind legs

There was a large gray animal he called a painted elephant on which sat a maharaja resplendent with the finest robes and jewels. The maharaja wore a large white turban on his head. There were beautiful ladies sitting beside him. This cloth was my treasure from him.

He told me of the aromatic spices the caravans brought to the merchants.

Sometimes the caravans got lost in the desert wandering in search of the precious water that was only in the oasis along the way. He said he had seen the skeletons of large tall camels that once carried the goods. They could last longer than any man walking in the desert he told me.

I pretended in my mind he and I were traveling in the desert back to the land of the golden tiger and painted elephant. He was the maharaja and I was one of the beautiful ladies sitting beside him. Then I could be with him forever.

The horses were slow going down the hill and into the snow covered valley. They gingerly treaded around the rocky ground. The snow had continued to fall all night and was deep in areas. The sun would cause some of it to melt making it more dangerous for the horses when the cold returned at night.

I wondered what shelter we could find at nightfall. As we came into a flat clearing he turned to me and said we must hurry now.

Jackie, a foreign-service officer, met us in Datong at the train station and escorted us to our new homes. The drive from the train station to the campus made me realize how large the city is with several million people. This one city had more people than the entire southeastern part of the United States where I had lived previously.

My new apartment was ideal. It had three bedrooms and a large kitchen. I was very happy in it.

Parts of the university were undergoing construction. It was twice the size of my last university in student population. The campus was big and still growing.

Nick's apartment was a little distance away. Federico had stayed at the train station to try and buy his tickets to his next destination. He would join us later that day.

He kindly had bought me a cell phone since my apartment phone was not working. It was generous of him to help me with it since I had no idea what type to get. I wanted something inexpensive. I was worried Sammy's habits were paying off finally. I could never admit it to him though. I would email him my new cell phone number.

It was so much cooler than in Hubei. We didn't need an air conditioner. I would have to write and tell Sammy about that for sure I thought. Hubei truly is the furnace of China in summer months. This was a wonderful change.

We went back into town for supper that night. Coming back home I realized how exhausted I was. Federico was staying with Nick until he left. I put new sheets on the bed and crawled in quickly. The new bed was so comfortable it only took minutes for me to fall asleep.

The horses snorted heavily as we picked up speed through the valley. It was cold. The snow was deep, and it was difficult for them to run there.

After we cleared the valley area we saw a small village on the side of the mountain. He said we must go on. There was no time to stop for food or shelter now.

We made our way past the village and up into the mountains again. This slowed the horses down. From the up high we would be able to see the guards coming. My horse was having difficulty climbing up the steep and slippery slopes.

He turned to me and said we must walk the horses for some time. My shoes sank into the snow. My robe became wet up to my knees. My cloth shoes were soaking wet. I could not stop shaking. My feet felt frozen. I slipped once and fell against the snow covered bank. My robe froze stiffly as I tried to walk.

An abandoned hut was within sight after we passed a grove of pine trees on top of a ridge. He motioned me to the house as he led the horses around to the back. I waited outside shivering as he tended to them.

There was a small space for them to be sheltered from any snow that night.

Federico and I went sightseeing in Datong. He had been there before and knew about some of the historical places in the city. He pointed out the huge rammed wall section made of earth many feet thick that was the city wall centuries before..

We spent a day wondering through a beautiful monastery that was a centuries old. I had never seen such beautiful statues, carvings, or paintings that existed inside the buildings within the monastery. I saw a monk dressed as they did centuries before.

Within two weeks Sammy came to visit. I was hoping he wouldn't worry about me once he saw my apartment and the school. Nick's apartment was being changed so they moved him in with me too for a week during that time.

Federico had left to travel in Inner Mongolia by this time. He jokingly emailed that my desire to have an apartment to myself seemed to be elusive for the moment. I missed him.

As Sammy and I lay talking in bed at night I realized how much I had missed him too. His being with me helped me to feel cared for and protected.

He helped me find a driver to take me to some private classes I taught. All the roads leading to or from the campus were under construction. The path changed daily. It was almost impossible to find drivers in town willing to travel to the university even though it was only a few miles from town.

For the month he stayed I don't recall dreaming at all. He played basketball and went swimming during that time. He had taken some swimming lessons after I left.

The previous year he and I went swimming in the hot springs in Xianning. That was his first adventure swimming then. Now he was very good at it, and wanted to practice. He was becoming more interested in athletics. I always told him I liked a man with muscles. I bought him his first basketball which seemed sad to me that he never had one as a child. When he left I gave it to the little boy next door.

Classes for the fall term began. It was a busy time getting settled into a routine. I was to teach the sophomores so my classes began as soon as school started.

The freshman students in China use the first month for their basic military training. They begin their classes after the National Day holiday which is the first week in October. I also taught four freshman classes.

The college in Xianning had not been able to replace my employment visa after my passport had been reissued so they changed it to a visitor visa. I would need to leave the country and apply for another one.

They had offered to extend my contract for a third year. As tempting as it was to stay there with Sammy for another year I felt it was time to leave. There was so much more of China I wanted to see, and wasn't sure how long they would let me teach in the country.

The school in Datong was concerned if I left and went home during the summer it may be more difficult to come back with the flu situation. So I came to Datong directly from Xianning. In July, I applied for an extension until the university in Datong could arrange for the work permit and letter of invitation to be issued.

With the A/H1N1 influenza pandemic going on, the work permits were delayed.

I was very nervous about my visa expiring even if it was the incorrect status. The school gave me an official letter stating that it was in process in case I was ever asked for my papers. Once the letter of invitation was issued I could leave and get the new visa.

During the National Day holiday the first week of October Sammy came back to visit. So we had one month apart. A student that Federico had introduced me to previously invited Sammy and me to go with him to visit another city in the same province.

We were to be guests of a government official whose son attended the university. I had met the son one evening before Sammy arrived.

The hotel accommodations, food and admissions were taken care of by the boy's parents. They invited us to their home. It was on the fourth floor of a new apartment complex. It was immaculate. The mother was most gracious serving all types of fruits. The father joined us and invited us to supper.

Before supper we had gone to see a park in the community. It was the burial park of an architect who had built a dam to save the people from the flooding each year. We were the only visitors that afternoon. It was peaceful and quite beautiful. The numerous pine trees and the smell reminded me of Christmas time.

Meals, important meals, are quite elaborate with numerous dishes. Many toasts are made to all parties. Meals are not about eating, but honoring those present. The host brought several bottles of wine which we all enjoyed. The food was beautiful and delicious.

The host went over to a flower arrangement and presented me with some of the flowers. It was a sweet thing for him to do. This was shortly after he asked another student there if I was a spy from America.

The mother, father, and sister spoke very little English. The college students who joined us, and Sammy and I conversed in English while the boys spoke to the family in Chinese.

The next day we were to climb a mountain and see many temples. Sammy never really liked being a tourist so I was concerned if he would get bored. Surprisingly, he liked the mountain adventure.

He and I took our second annual cable car ride. He reminded me it was only a year ago since we had gone to Wudang. I told him we would have to do this somewhere in the world each October. I sang on the way up which made him nervous. He asked me to be still and not talk.

After reaching the platform from the cable car there are still about thousand steps to reach all the temples on the mountain. They cannot be seen from the ground easily and the design affords them extreme protection from the elements and possible invaders in the past. The buildings date back centuries. Monks still live in the complex. One showed me how to walk at a slanted angle up the very steepest steps.

There is something magical and spiritual about the mountains in China. They possess the spirit or the charm of things ancient and sacred.

Each October as I visit one I think nothing can be more beautiful and each year I am surprised.

At the highest point and temple on the mountain monks were playing ancient musical instruments. It was amazingly peaceful.

That afternoon we went to the Suspending Temple in another area of the province a short distance away. It is also a protected UNESCO site with guards present to protect this valuable piece of history and relic of ancient China. It is a centuries old temple clinging to the side of a mountain rock. It is a engineering feat unequaled anywhere else in the world.

It took almost an hour to climb up the steep steps to the temple. The depth in between each step is much steeper than you can imagine. Sammy almost had to pull me up between stairs. The steps are very short in space making it difficult to place your foot firmly on each step. The stairways are extremely narrow and you must bend over to climb up.

When you look out from the balconies you realize the monks did this for centuries. We were able to see exactly what they saw so long ago. They were and are safe here.

The next morning we visited another temple complex being restored within the city. It has been hidden away and is a secret to most. Local town people have been the guardians of this gem. As I walked into the courtyard you can see the most beautiful bouquets of flowers fading that must have bloomed earlier in the summer.

The colors are still there in random flowers still blooming. A monk was painting to restore a building. Huge plaster or clay figures of deities donned in warrior garb sit stately inside one building. In another temple women go to pray for a boy while they are pregnant. The deities in there are covered in red veils.

I wanted to buy some religious posters similar to those I had seen in the temples. One of the students knew the shops where they were sold and we went to buy them before lunch. After a delicious luncheon where the student's mother and sister joined us we left for home.

Sammy left for home the day after we got back. Finding transportation anywhere during the holiday was difficult. The student that invited us on the trip, Jerry, had a friend who helped arrange the ticket. Without it Sammy would have had to stay in Datong because there were no flights or other trains available. Millions of people crowd the buses, trains, and airlines for travel during the holidays. China definitely moves during these times.

When he left I realized I needed some time alone just to be by myself. After so many days with people constantly with us or around I just needed to wear sloppy clothes and not put on makeup for a few days without anyone talking to me or staring at me. I jumped out of the fishbowl for a few days. It was heavenly.

Students often ask me if I am lonely. I respond it is difficult to be alone in China. Since it is the first time many of them have ever been away from their parents they are lonely and think I must be as well. I enjoy solitude at times. If I want to be around people I find them. When Sammy and I are together we adjust to each other's routines.

I slept for twenty four hours after he left. It felt as though a century had past when I woke up. I was carried through that century in my dreams.

> *The horses were sheltered and out of the weather in a stable behind the wooden hut.*
>
> *I was afraid to enter the hut alone. When he returned I was still standing there with my garments frozen around me. Never had I been so cold. The snow was getting deeper. It came up to just below my knees. If the snow did not stop it would not be possible to ride tomorrow through the valley. If we could not move neither could the soldiers either though.*
>
> *He helped me to move slowly into the old hut. I felt helpless like a child not knowing what to do. He took the fur around his shoulders and draped it around me. He pushed me to sit down on a bench. I stumbled onto the bench grabbing the fur and wrapping it tightly. He removed my cloth shoes. He pulled a long white turban from his pack and wrapped my feet in it.*

I could not feel anything. I could not even speak, and simply closed my eyes. I leaned back against the wall.

I heard the door shut on the hut. He had gone out. It seemed a long time before he returned. I must have slept. I could see daylight when he left, but it was dark when he returned. He had a load of firewood and had snared a rabbit. We would eat tonight.

There was a dirty pot he had filled with snow to wash out. Then he added fresh snow to melt for water. The fireplace glowed with the warmth of the fire he built quickly.

My feet and hands began to burn as sensations began to return. He was roasting the rabbit. I could smell the aroma of it cooking.

He poured me a gourd full of water from the pan. I drank it down slowly savoring every drop. Never before had I gone without water or food for so long. It was a strange feeling being so hungry and thirsty all at once. After I drank the water I was starving for the taste of the rabbit.

He broke off a leg and handed the simmering piece to me. It burned my lips with the heat, but I didn't care. I was eating. Without him I would have died from starvation or thirst. Without him I didn't want to live.

He sat by the fire enjoying the burnt rabbit pieces he tore from the roast stick. He looked up at me smiling. I am the hunter he laughed looking at me all the while.

After we had eaten we warmed ourselves by the fire. My clothes had began to dry. He left to check on the horses. He brought back a bag with clothing.

Handing some to me he turned his back so I could change into them. I unwrapped myself from the fur blanket and quickly slipped into them. I stepped into the long boots and pulled them up. I had never walked in anything like this before. He laughed at me and I tried to navigate around the room to get used to walking in them.

Now I looked like a common peasant. The fabric of the material was rough and coarse. It was much warmer than my silken gown had been though. I was grateful to him for it. If we could hide my long hair under a hat I could pass for a man now in his clothes.

He threw my gown and shoes into the fire. They smoldered for a few moments then burst into flames. I looked down at the piece of fabric in my hand. I had taken it out of a pocket in my gown before he tossed it into the fire. The beautiful colored scarf he had given me was the only part of my past that visibly remained. I folded it and put it into my vest so it would be safe again.

He had made a pallet on the floor next to the fire. Come and sleep he said. As I lay down he wrapped the fur blanket over us. Gently he put his arm around me and I slept. I could feel the warmth from his body. For the first time that day I was warm. I remember hearing him breathe heavily as he slept.

Within a week after Sammy left, the university canceled classes due to A/H1N1 flu. I was teaching a class when the monitor called female students, roommates of one of my students, out and told them to return to their dorm. One of the female students had a fever and they would confine them to the dorm until they could determine if she had A/H1N1.Within three days of the first reported cases the school closed.

I had gone to the school clinic the day the first case was reported for a seasonal flu shot. I wasn't aware at that time any students had it. It would not have been possible to get one after that because the clinic closed the next day due to the number of students arriving with fever.

The school issued a thermometer to the dorms for students to take their temperature each morning and afternoon. If they had fever they were to report to the school hospital. Then they were taken to a special dormitory for treatment. Serious cases were transferred outside. Free vaccinations were offered and I received one as a precaution.

Roommates were confined to the rooms. The atmosphere was tense. They were issued masks to wear and could not leave campus. There were all kinds of rumors. It was hard to know what was really happening.

By the fourth day over fifty students had reported fever. University students could not leave campus, but teachers could. Many did not live on campus. Also younger students, family members of teachers, who attended class in town still attended their schools since they were not closed. There were taxis and buses available to transport us for shopping or going to town.

I went to teach some private classes in town and also went to shop for groceries in the event we were confined to the school. Cleaning and watching television or working on the computer filled my time during these days. Sammy and I spoke or emailed daily. He was worried about what was happening.

During this time he was preparing for his student teaching assignment which he would do in November. Odom was back from India studying for his graduate work.

He and Sammy became friends during this time. Often Odom would stay over at his apartment. It seems funny to me they would become close friends after all.

Classes resumed after two weeks. The makeup schedule meant teaching six days a week to catch up on those classes missed.

In early November we had the first snowfall. When classes met again we had a very heavy snowfall. The news said it was the most snow northern China had seen since 1949. So we had students and teachers struggling to come to class in snow. If they weren't sick before then the change of weather wouldn't help at all.

The ice was dangerous on the roads. I managed to fall twice within a week, but didn't break anything. Both sides of my body were black and blue from falling on the ice. Some of my students had to leave school because of injuries when slipping on the icy roads. Students kindly tried to help me back and forth by walking with me.

Some nights I was exhausted simply from walking back from class. All I wanted to do was sleep. The dreams returned…..

> *We woke to a crashing sound. Tree branches were breaking off from the ice and snow falling to the ground. He went outside to check on the horses.*

I lay there under the fur not wanting to get up, but knew that I must do so. There was still a small fire and the small hut was warm.

I got up and cleaned myself up with melted snow water. I was stirring the fire when he came back in. He brought some wood he found in the shed where the horses were quartered. It was not quite daylight.

We warmed ourselves by the fire and drank tea for an hour before setting out for the day. He told me we must try and reach a mountain pass before nightfall. Once we made it to the pass we would be outside the realm of the warlord. Only then would I feel safe.

By midday we had been able to travel farther than in the past few days. The sun was shinning melting the snow. The horses sometimes had trouble keeping their footing in the snow as it disintegrated into slush and mud. But onward we rode.

We had past a few small villages, but skirted around them not stopping. At last we came upon a small inn when he told me we would go inside. The small old woman brought us soup and tea as we sat down at a rough wooden table. There was a fire close by and the warmth kept my teeth from chattering. We ate without talking.

He asked the old woman if there had been any other travelers stopping recently. She said some guards from the warlord's household had come by that morning, but had turned back and returned in the direction they had come from in the east.

We had not passed any as we rode that day. The path we took was not on the road, but riding the ridge of the mountains until we came through the narrow pass.

We were free of the guards. We were free to begin another life together.

The semester came to an end. It took me several weeks testing daily to get all my students tested orally before I could do grades.

During this time I also went to Bangkok to get my visa status changed. The first time I tried the Beijing immigration police stopped me from getting on the airplane saying my visa had expired. They were not impressed with the documentation from the university. Being detained by the police was a frightening experience.

The officer yelled at me I should be able to speak Chinese better if I wanted to live in China he said. That was not a requirement to teach at the university. I have enough presence of mind to act respectfully. Finally, after my flight had departed without me they let me go, and had two policemen escorted me out of the terminal. I have never even had a parking ticket so I was definitely shaken.

Without Sammy's help I would not have been able to find a place to stay that night. You have to have a valid visa to stay in a hotel. He stayed on the phone with me to make sure I had enough money, enough money on my phone, and got me a hotel room through a friend. He talked to the taxi drivers to guide me and translate. He was simply amazing.

He had his friend pick me up from hotel the next morning and took me to the train station making sure I got on at the right time and into the right sleeper bed. He had also sent money overnight to his friend's account so I could have extra money in case I needed it. I felt drained and worried about what would happen when I got back to Datong to had to report to the police station there.

I text the foreign service contact and explained what happened and asked that he accompany me the next day to the police station to resolve the situation. We went and met with the police commissioner who explained I had broken the law and there could be a significant fine for the expired visa. I explained what happened as they took my statement. I was not arrested. The police commissioner called the foreign-service person that evening and said there would be no fine.

We were contacted to return to the police station about a week later for the final hearing. There I received a warning. I was told that my visa was invalid and a new one would be issued so I could leave and get the proper visa type out of country.

Another week later I had my passport with a temporary visa. I made reservations to leave for Bangkok within three days. The yearlong nightmare of having my passport stolen, being issued a tourist replacement visa instead of a work visa, being detained by the Beijing police, and finally being able to leave the country was over. Things were about to be cleared up at last.

I fell in love with Bangkok when I finally arrived there. People put their hands together in the form of praying to say thank you and hello as a sign of respect. There are huge posters of the king posted on every highway, on the money and inside every building.

Street after street has thousands of vendors setting up stalls on the sidewalk selling beautiful fabrics and clothing. You can smell the delicious food sold by sidewalk vendors as you walk by trying to take in all the colors, and sights around you. Everything is green, blooming, and hot compared to China which had snow when I left. The streets never close. Partying goes on in the streets as well as eating until early morning hours. Bangkok offers something for everyone.

I was able to get the visa in one day, and a physical exam in one hour. The hospital was modern, clean and the personnel and doctor were fast and efficient. It was incredibly inexpensive to obtain the health certificate and physical. Reassured that I was in fairly good health I shopped until I dropped.

New Year's Eve I was in the airport waiting for my flight. I wished the Chinese immigration happy new year as I was whisked back into the country. I was legal, and after a train ride was home again finally.

It snowed my first night home. I awoke to a beautiful white world to start off the year. Sammy would be arriving soon to spend the holiday. He had asked me to spend the summer with him, and maybe I would.

The university foreign service office personnel had asked me to stay and teach for another year. So I would stay in Datong for awhile longer.

Sammy and I must have lived before I think in other times and places. I am only conscious that now we have met again in this time in this incredible place called China. Never before have I believed in reincarnation. I will never really know the truth. I only know to trust the dreams.

The end is no where in sight.

www.ingramcontent.com/pod-product-compliance
Ingram Content Group UK Ltd.
Pitfield, Milton Keynes, MK11 3LW, UK
UKHW041835200726
13854UKWH00003BA/1141